BIBLE READING

• FROM BRF •

FOR THE
CHRISTMAS SEASON

Text copyright © BRF 2002

Published by
The Bible Reading Fellowship
First Floor, Elsfield Hall
15–17 Elsfield Way, Oxford OX2 8FG
ISBN 1 84101 311 0

First published 2002
10 9 8 7 6 5 4 3 2 1 0

Acknowledgments
Unless otherwise stated, scripture quotations are taken from the *Holy Bible, New International Version*, copyright © 1973, 1978, 1984 by International Bible Society, and are used by permission of Hodder & Stoughton Limited. All rights reserved. 'NIV' is a registered trademark of International Bible Society. UK trademark number 1448790.

Scripture quotations taken from The New Revised Standard Version of the Bible, Anglicized Edition, copyright © 1989, 1995 by the Division of Christian Education of the National Council of the Churches of Christ in the USA, are used by permission. All rights reserved.

The Holy Bible, New King James Version, copyright © 1982 by Thomas Nelson, Inc.

A catalogue record for this book is available from the British Library

Printed and bound in Great Britain by
Bookmarque, Croydon

CONTENTS

GENERAL INTRODUCTION

Welcome to the Christmas edition of BRF's Bible reading sampler. We think you'll find something to enjoy here, whether it's a taste of our regular Bible reading notes, an extract from one of our *People's Bible Commentary volumes*, or simply finding out more about the range of publications that we produce.

At BRF we are passionate about helping people grow in personal Bible reading and prayer, as well as in being a member of the Christian Church. By reading the Bible, we grow in the knowledge of how our faith fits together, and this nurtures our prayer life, both as individuals and as worshipping communities. And reading with the help of insightful comment from others can help us get deeper into God's word, challenge our assumptions and bring us fresh insights into familiar passages.

Naomi Starkey

Naomi Starkey
Managing Editor, Bible reading notes

DAY BY DAY
WITH GOD

Bible Readings for Women

Day by Day with God (published jointly with Christina Press) is written especially by women for women, with a regular team of contributors. Each four-monthly issue offers daily Bible readings, with key verses printed out, helpful comment and a prayer for the day ahead. Our *Day by Day with God* extract contains readings for Christmas and the New Year and comes from Elaine Pountney, on the theme 'Journey to a different land' (from the September–December 2002 notes), and Diana Archer, on the theme 'Moses'. Elaine Pountney works with IFES (International Fellowship of Evangelical Students) Eurasia senior leadership team as a consultant and co-ordinator of the work among Christian students in Ukraine and Moldova. Diana Archer works with the Damaris Trust in Southampton, producing home-group Bible studies on the Internet.

Journeys 'to' are journeys 'away from'

Jesus replied: 'A certain man was preparing a great banquet and invited many guests… "Come, for everything is now ready." … Still another said, "I just got married, so I can't come."'

We had packed and tightly taped the last of the boxes that held basic household necessities for moving to and living in an old Soviet apartment block in Ukraine. We were embarking on an adventure, a journey. Suddenly our home in Canada looked better than ever, glowing with comfort, 'known-ness' and beauty.

I was finding it hard to imagine what living in an apartment in Ukraine was really going to be like. We had been warned that hot water and electricity would be intermittent and possibly non-existent for extended periods of times. But worse than that, we would miss our family and friends! We would miss pushing our beautiful granddaughters on the swings. We would miss candle-lit meals together with friends and family. We would miss deep conversation over dark cappuccinos.

But we had been invited to share a banquet of ministry that was taking place in Ukraine and Moldova—and everything was ready! 'But our friends and family are here,' we were tempted to protest. 'Our grandchildren are here. We can't come just now.'

It makes me wonder how Mary managed her journey from anonymity into being 'highly favoured by God'. Mary had not only become pregnant in a most unorthodox way, but she required personal protection by the man she was promised to in marriage. Her life journey took her away from respectability, from cultural acceptance and from the normative comfort of her home.

In the middle of all these losses, where was her journey taking her? To a great banquet that was now ready! To the birth of a king whose journey would take him from majesty to humanity, from glory to a woman's womb, from splendour to a stable.

And Mary delighted in being invited to such a banquet and on such a journey.

Dear Jesus, give us Mary-hearts that are willing to journey from our places of comfort to the great banquet that is ready—now.

EP

Luke 14:15–24 (NIV)

Journey to the banquet

Jesus replied: 'A certain man was preparing a great banquet and invited many guests... "Come, for everything is now ready." ... Another said, "I have just bought five yoke of oxen, and I'm on my way to try them out. Please excuse me."'

An unexpected conversation with a young man in a waiting-room— and an even more unexpected story. He is a young Ukrainian, waiting to speak with someone about a job. In conversation he tells us how, a year ago, he had a very successful marketing job. But he is now unemployed, penniless, wondering what he is going to do, struggling with a call to become a pastor.

In the job he used to have, his boss would give him a suitcase full of money to wine and dine prospective clients, to take them to the local brothels. His boss's instructions were, 'Give them a good time.' And if he closed a deal, his commission would be about $40,000. This young committed Christian protested, 'I can't do that. I'm a Christian.' And the consequence? He is no longer employed.

In biblical terms, this young man chose to go to the banquet and not to go and take care of his own oxen first. He has been forced to choose: economic security in a fragile economy, or the poverty of faithfulness. He made a courageous choice. Have you ever had to make such choices—when to choose God and his banquet is to say goodbye to assured wealth and security?

Mary and Joseph had a similar choice: would Joseph choose Mary or abandon her in her unusual pregnancy? Would he choose the cultural route or would he listen to the angel messenger? To listen to the angel would complicate their lives considerably, but it would also bring a joy beyond their imagining. And they would be blessed.

God, do the choices have to be so hard? Give us gifts of grace and courage to choose the banquet and leave our oxen behind.

EP

Luke 9:57–62 (NIV)

Journey with a companion

As they were walking along the road, a man said to him, 'I will follow you wherever you go.' … Jesus replied, 'No one who puts his hand to the plough and looks back is fit for service in the kingdom of God.'

All I wanted to do was to go home! This wasn't what I had expected following Jesus to be about. I had been invited here to do a particular job and now that job had clearly been taken away. I thought it was time that God started explaining some things to me. I had kept my part of the agreement and had followed him, but now the rug had been pulled out from under my feet. Didn't God have a responsibility in our agreement?

I clearly had a bone to pick with God on this one. I was angry with certain people who, from my perspective, had broken promises. I felt misused. I felt that God had taken a vacation and I was stranded here with a multi-year commitment!

When I stopped ranting, and listened long enough to hear God, I heard his gentle words of love. Underneath my hurt and my anger was fear—fear that I had wrongly heard the call to follow; fear that God had forgotten that I was a stranger here, trying to follow him; fear that somehow I had really messed up and that I deserved being abandoned!

When I listened, I heard him encourage me to keep my hand on the plough—right next to his. He was guiding the plough; his was the power that kept it steady. I just needed to walk alongside him. Even the tears that filled my eyes wouldn't cancel the call if I simply walked alongside him. And although I wanted to turn back and go home, I didn't. I'm still walking alongside him.

Mary and Joseph must have wanted to turn back many times when the journey was hard, when the journey didn't seem to make sense, when they felt alone. But they kept their hands to the plough and followed where Jesus' journey needed to go.

Thank you, Jesus, that your hand is on the plough right next to mine.
EP

Luke 2:4–7 (NIV)

Journeys through difficulty

So Joseph also went up from the town of Nazareth in Galilee to Judea, to Bethlehem the town of David… While they were there, the time came for the baby to be born.

Do you notice how often our journeys to follow God happen at the most inopportune time?

We can imagine the excitement of Mary and Joseph after the visit of the angels, and the liveliness of their long conversations, trying to make sense of the strange events in their lives—the way their journey was unfolding. How would a young couple talk about conversations with angels and about the expected birth of God's Son? And then for Mary to find herself in the discomfort of the final days of her pregnancy travelling a long distance only to discover Bethlehem overcrowded and its inns full… well, it sure would make me stop and think about where God was in all this! But Mary seemed to ponder these things in her heart, waiting for God to give her an understanding of all these strange events in her life that were designed by God.

Mary's and Joseph's journeys were custom-designed to achieve God's purposes and plans for them, as are ours. But life's journeys are not without difficulty and challenge. Just think back on your own journeys amid your own difficult times. How seldom we really know ahead of time what God's design looks like, and how much, at times, we long to know what is coming. How surprised we are as we see how our faithful God moulds and shapes us through the difficulties. Yet each difficulty is a potential birth, an opportunity for something new to be born within us—the formation of new attitudes, new understanding, new commitment, the knowledge of God himself.

God, give us faith and hope and understanding when the difficulties in our journey seem to be pointless. Help us to have eyes to see the possibilities of each situation—especially the difficult ones.

EP

Luke 2:1–7 (NIV)

Journey to register

In those days Caesar Augustus issued a decree that a census should be taken of the entire Roman world... So Joseph also went up from the town of Nazareth in Galilee to Judea, to Bethlehem... He went there to register with Mary.

We were off to the train station to buy train tickets to Simferopol, a city in Crimea—but still in Ukraine. We weren't crossing any borders, so we were a bit surprised when we were asked to show our passports. Later, when we bought plane tickets, we were again asked to show our passports. We weren't used to having to prove who we were for these 'non-passport' activities.

When we asked our friends in Crimea why we needed to do that each time, they pulled their own registration cards out of their pockets and explained that they carry their cards with them all the time. Citizens in the old Soviet empire still do not have complete freedom to move around their own country. They can be stopped at any time and asked by the military to show their registration cards, or risk being taken away for questioning. Their registration cards are proof that they have the right to move and go about their daily business where they are. So now we carry our passports containing our visas with us all the time. It feels strange but they provide the documentation that we have been given permission to be here in this country. They are our identity and our registration here.

Mary and Joseph's journey took them away from Nazareth back to Bethlehem to register—Rome had decreed it. Joseph was required to register in Bethlehem, his ancestral home. Who is Joseph? Oh, he belongs to David's family. Who is Mary? She's pledged to Joseph in marriage. Who are you and who am I? We are registered to God's family, in the kingdom of God. And our passports have a visa stamped with God's seal of ownership upon us: we have his Spirit in our hearts (2 Corinthians 1:21).

Thank you, Father, that we belong in your kingdom.

EP

Journey of pain

Then Simeon blessed them and said to Mary, his mother:
'…And a sword will pierce your own soul too.'

One minute apart: the contractions were becoming stronger and were coming more rapidly. I was trying to encourage my daughter to keep focused on her breathing exercises and to be strong with the increasing pain. During the pain of the contractions, we both seemed to lose sight of the anticipated joy in the imminent arrival of little Jessica. As the new life of the little baby getting ready to burst into this world got closer, the pain got stronger.

We had been waiting for this moment since three o'clock in the morning—walking around the hospital, sipping juice, talking, clocking contractions—and now, finally, the birth was close. Yet each contraction in itself seemed like an eternity—like it might never end—as we waited and wondered if her husband would actually make it to the hospital before the baby was born, hoping but not sure he would arrive.

Sitting with my daughter through the early hours of the morning gave me an opportunity to think about how pain and anticipated joy inseparably weave themselves together to form a predictable pattern in our journey—and how good it was just to be with my daughter, knowing that giving birth to this little baby was her work, not mine. Mine was simply to walk alongside her, to be there with her until her husband arrived.

It also gave me an opportunity to wonder imaginatively: was Jesus' Father pacing the corridors of heaven watching his son being born in the natural pangs of childbirth? Was he anxious? I wonder if Mary had a sense of her son's heavenly Father being present, encouraging and blessing. And did it reduce the pain? I expect not, because right from the beginning Mary's journey was a mixture of experienced pain—pain far greater than that of childbirth—and anticipated joy. Our journey is the same.

God, give us grace never to lose sight of the wonder and the anticipation of joy as we see you daily brought to birth in new ways; and give us grace to be strong in those times of pain.

EP

Journey with grace

*'I am the Lord's servant,' Mary answered. 'May it be to me
as you have said.'*

It was an old pattern, quickly recognized, but it got me stuck again.
I was fighting with the need to be acknowledged and recognized
for my contribution—my old Achilles' heel, as my husband said. I
was invited to participate, I did my work, and then I was sidelined.
I really struggle with situations like this. Something gets triggered
deep inside of me. It's as if I am fighting for my very life: it's a
suffocating feeling of panic.

At such times, I have heated internal arguments with God,
almost demanding that he goes and changes *their* behaviour instead
of asking *me* to find a holy attitude—like, why isn't it *their* turn to
learn something, instead of *mine* again! I get quite discouraged
because I have so often asked God to give me a gentle, kind
forgiveness for these colleagues—to heal my Achilles' heel.

So I am profoundly moved when I read Mary's beautiful and
simple response to an angel's visit: 'I am the Lord's servant. May it
be to me as you have said.' 'Whatever, God—I trust you with my
life,' she's saying. She shows such grace and responsiveness to God's
plan for her life.

However, she was greatly troubled by the angel Gabriel's opening
comments, 'Greetings, you who are highly favoured! The Lord is
with you.' This greeting seemed to unnerve her, perhaps because
she had an immediate, intuitive understanding that along with such
a greeting there must be mysterious implications that would
profoundly impact her own life. She was a wise woman in her youth.
But still, she bowed to the circumstances that God's plan would
bring into her life.

As my journey continues to unfold, I'd like to be as full of grace
in response to the circumstances of my life as Mary was in hers.

---

*Jesus, give me grace to be full of gentle Mary-grace as I journey
with you.*

EP

Luke 2:6–7 (NIV)

Journey into life

*While they were there, the time came for the baby to be born, and
she gave birth to her firstborn, a son. She wrapped him in cloths
and placed him in a manger, because there was no room for them
in the inn.*

Finally! It was time for little Jessica to be born! My daughter was
pushing and Jessica was already emerging. This was the moment
we had all been waiting for. It was time. With a final big push,
little Jessica was born, kicking and breathing, totally dependent
and totally beautiful.

Then it was time to cut the umbilical cord and she was released
into this world to begin her journey. The first happening on her
journey was to get a big hug and kiss from her mum and hear
whispers of, 'You're beautiful. I love you', then more hugs and kisses.

As the more practical things like measuring, weighing and
checking Jessica out physically were happening, I was struck with
the wonder that I had been watching 'my baby' give birth to 'her
baby'. It did make me wonder what it is like for God as he gives new
birth and new life to us when we believe in Jesus. Does he feel the
same wonder and privilege and joy? I can't help but think that he
does. Does he feel birthpangs as we become believers? I don't know,
but I do know that I would love to have been present when Mary
gave birth to Jesus and to have wondered with her about giving
birth to the Son of God. I expect it would have been similar to
having shared the experience with my daughter. I expect I would
have heard an earthly mother and father, along with a heavenly
Father, whispering, 'You're beautiful. I love you.'

And if we stop long enough to listen, I expect we would hear
our heavenly Father singing to us in whispers, 'You're beautiful.
I love you.'

---

*Jesus, thank you for life and thank you that we have been born again
in you.*

EP

Luke 2:15–16 (NIV)

Worship with unlikely people

When the angels had left them and gone into heaven, the shepherds said to one another, 'Let's go to Bethlehem and see this thing that has happened, which the Lord has told us about.' So they hurried off and found Mary and Joseph, and the baby, who was lying in the manger.

Two hours after Jessica had been born, her father came bounding into the room, having just arrived from the airport. He had missed Jessica's birth because she had decided to arrive considerably earlier than expected. Life is like that, isn't it? It just isn't under our control.

It was fun watching him express his joy in his wife and new daughter. In fact, I felt as if I was intruding in a very intimate moment. So before I went off to get a coffee and leave them alone for a moment, I got swept up into the precious gift of love and affection that he was pouring out on his family.

The next visitor who was a delight to watch was Jessica's two-year-old sister, who arrived with her grandad. She walked right up to her mum, patted her tummy, said, 'Baby out', marched over to baby Jessica in her daddy's arms and gave her a big hug and kiss. Grandad, meanwhile, simply beamed from the foot of the bed, enjoying his family and oozing love and joy.

I feel that God the Father must have beamed with similar delight as he began to tell people of his Son's birth. Out in the fields, he told a bunch of shepherds who were quite startled to be informed! What unlikely people to find God inviting to the birth of his Son. But having watched Jessica's dad and her grandad beaming and sharing the news with anyone who would listen, I think Jesus' heavenly Father just couldn't keep it to himself.

As at Jesus' birth, we will find the most unlikely people sharing our journey with us. I'm sure Mary was as surprised as we are to see who God brought into the birthing room. But then, that's just like our heavenly Father, don't you think?

EP

Luke 2:10–11 (NIV)

Journey of promise

'I bring you good news of great joy that will be for all the people.
Today in the town of David a Saviour has been born to you;
he is Christ the Lord.'

Baby Jessica is now a few months old. When she was safely growing in her mother's womb in her initial months of life, she was unseen, a promise of a life to come—a promise that God had plans and purpose for her and that those plans were good. Having now been born, she is known and seen, and greatly loved. All the possibilities and promise of life are being realized in a happy, churgling-gurgling-cooing baby.

For hundreds of years, there were promises of a Messiah, one who would save his people; and now, held in the arms of Mary and Joseph, those promises were becoming a reality. 'Today'—today—'in the town of David a Saviour has been born to you; he is Christ the Lord,' the angels told the shepherds. He has arrived: he has come—no longer just a promise, for the Shepherds saw him and heard him. They had worshipped him! And the skies were filled with angels who also saw and heard the King of kings churgling, gurgling and cooing. They joined the shepherds in praise and worship of this king.

And Mary 'treasured up all these things and pondered them in her heart... And the child grew and became strong; he was filled with wisdom, and the grace of God was upon him' (Luke 2:20, 40)—just as it was promised!

God, the maker and keeper of promises, still meets us today, giving us hope in his promises of life. So we have the possibility of journeying with God who takes the promises out of the future tense of anticipation and puts them into the past tense of our experience. Like Mary, we can ponder these things in our hearts.

Lord Jesus, change your promises for our future into the past tense of our experience. Teach us also to treasure these things and ponder them in our heart.

EP

Exodus 1:15–17 (NIV)

Start with Moses

The king of Egypt said to the Hebrew midwives, whose names were Shiphrah and Puah, 'When you help the Hebrew women in childbirth and observe them on the delivery stool, if it is a boy, kill him; but if it is a girl, let her live.' The midwives, however, feared God and did not do what the king of Egypt had told them to do; they let the boys live.

A new day, a new year, a new start. For those of us adept at muddling through life, we hope that perhaps this year we will be more ordered. Perhaps our walk with God will be more like a Roman road heading for heaven and less like a meandering country lane where we lose our perspective at every turn. So, where to start? Sorting the socks or two hours in prayer? Is that the telephone ringing? Oh, what does it matter anyway?

For all those unrealistic, easily-distracted dreamers out there like me, look at Shiphrah and Puah. We meet these two women at the start of the story of Moses, even before he was born. They were squashed between two male-dominated societies, with one, Egypt, enslaving the other, Israel. These midwives had no status, but the Bible singles them out because their actions were vital. Despite their vulnerability, they chose civil disobedience. By saving the boys' lives, they had a profound impact on the whole Hebrew nation, preventing its emasculation. What would have happened otherwise?

How did they change the course of history? By fearing God and doing their job well. Because God was the defining priority in their lives, they chose to obey him rather than Pharaoh. They continued to perform their job with integrity and to respect the sanctity of life. Thus they saved a nation.

Whatever your situation this New Year, be encouraged. You matter to God and your choices count. They may not have nation-saving status, but God can use everything.

Dear Father, teach me how to fear you, and help me to do my job well. Amen.

Read Lamentations 3:22–26.

DA

Exodus 1:18b–21 (NIV)

Superwomen

'Why have you done this? Why have you let the boys live?' The midwives answered Pharaoh, 'Hebrew women are not like Egyptian women; they are vigorous and give birth before the midwives arrive.' So God was kind to the midwives and the people increased and became even more numerous. And because the midwives feared God, he gave them families of their own.

Day Two. New Year. I hope the novelty hasn't worn off yet. Seize the day!

As we dive into the early years of Moses' life, these prep-aratory events set the scene. Guess what—they all revolve around women! It is women who are the key players in this unfolding drama. Without these wonderful midwives, where would the Hebrew men have been? Now Shiphrah and Puah are face to face with Pharaoh. Was this a downright lie—that they never got to the action in time? Did the Hebrew women give birth faster than the Egyptians, so that this was just stretching the truth a little? Certainly the midwives must have been in league with the mothers, together determined to protect the innocent baby boys. For those of us who have borne children, the thought of doing so in such difficult circumstances is awesome. Was it really a case of, 'Push, push—before the midwives get here!'?

Whatever went on, it was the women who saved the day. They took incredible risks to protect human life. Their actions reflect those of all who, down the centuries, have tried to sabotage genocide. The biblical account here reiterates what motivated Shiphrah and Puah—the fear of the Lord.

'Fearing God' is not a phrase I hear very often. No one lately has asked me if I fear God. What does it mean, if it led these women into potential danger? It also led them to care for others. Where does the fear of the Lord lead you and me? Is God really number one in our lives, so that we will willingly follow that leading?

Lord, help me to be whole-hearted in following you. Amen.

DA

Exodus 2:3b–4 (NIV)

Moses afloat

She got a papyrus basket for [Moses] and coated it with tar and pitch. Then she placed the child in it and put it among the reeds along the bank of the Nile. His sister stood at a distance to see what would happen to him.

New Year day three. How many resolutions have flown out the window? Isn't it wonderful that God deals in grace?

Anyone who has been to a Sunday school worth its salt will be very familiar with the story of Moses. You have probably made/ drawn/painted this very scene—a cute three-month-old gurgling in a miniature boat. Revisiting the plot with a more 'grown up' perspective adds depth to the drama.

It is the women again. Desperate to thwart Pharaoh's evil edict that all baby boys must now be thrown into the Nile, Moses' mother plans a possible escape. Moses' basket is placed near the princess's bathing haunt—surely this was strategic? Moses' sister is set on watch. How many nights had Moses' mother lain awake worrying before hitting on this idea? Her ingenuity had kept Moses alive so far. Would this new risk prove worth taking? In order to stand any chance of saving him, she had to give up her son.

All of us face impossible situations at some times in our lives. Finding the courage and imagination to face our problems is no easier for us than for these heroines of the Old Testament. Moses' mother's response was vital for the future of a nation. I am sure it was also heart-rending. The situations we face may demand equivalent courage and sacrifice. It is often so hard to know what to do, or how to find the strength to do it. How can we be wise?

We are back to the fear of the Lord again—for that, according to Psalm 111:10, is the beginning of wisdom.

A reminder: God grant me the serenity to accept the things I cannot change, the courage to change the things I can, and the wisdom to know the difference.

DA

Exodus 2:5–6 (NIV)

Nile discovery

Pharaoh's daughter... saw the basket... She opened it and saw the baby. He was crying, and she felt sorry for him. 'This is one of the Hebrew babies,' she said.

Here we go again—God's plan for a whole nation being achieved through women. This time, a privileged young woman took pity on a helpless, doomed child. Pharaoh's daughter did not have to choose compassion: she could easily have ordered a servant to tip the basket into the river and gone back to painting her toenails. But no, it seems this lady had an inherited stubborn streak. Never mind that Daddy had a large political headache because of the Hebrews multiplying in his country. Never mind that in rescuing this Hebrew baby she was directly contradicting his orders. Her instinctive compassion was the overriding factor. Yet again, Pharaoh was to be outwitted by a determined woman who valued human life.

It is, of course, wonderfully ironic that Moses' mother was paid to nurse her own son, and that Moses was brought up with all the privileges of a princess's son, right under the nose of the enemy. He was even given an Egyptian name. Moses was being well grounded in the ways of the Egyptian court—knowledge he would draw on in his later vocation.

Sometimes it is impossible to see how God may be at work in situations, whether personal or political. The Israelites had to suffer and struggle in slavery for many more years before Moses came back to rescue them. But the plan was there, all the time, quietly growing in Pharaoh's own household, despite his futile attempts to quash God's people.

Next time you are tempted to think that God has forgotten you, or lost the plot somewhere, remember the story of Moses. God's timing or methods may not be the ones we would choose, but they are there nevertheless. Remember too, the privilege of being a woman. Without women, Moses never would have been.

'God is working his purpose out as year succeeds to year...'
ARTHUR CAMPBELL AINGER (1841–1919)

DA

Guidelines

Guidelines is a unique Bible reading resource that offers four months of in-depth study written by leading scholars. Contributors are drawn from around the world as well as the UK, and represent a stimulating and thought-provoking breadth of Christian tradition. Instead of dated daily readings, *Guidelines* provides weekly units, broken into at least six sections, plus an introduction giving context for the passage, and a final section of points for thought and prayer. On any day you can read as many or as few sections as you wish. As well as a copy of *Guidelines*, you will need a Bible, as the passage is not included. The *Guidelines* extract in this sampler, on the theme 'Songs of Glory', is by Anne Stevens, who is priest-in-charge of St Michael's, Battersea, and Director of Reader Training for the Diocese of Southwark.

Songs of Glory

Praise the Lord! How good it is to sing praises to our God. (Psalm 147:1)

At this time of year, thousands of people will discover this for themselves in churches all round the world. The familiar songs of Christmas can seem trite and meaningless when we hear them in a supermarket or on a TV advert. But when we sing them in a carol service or a packed midnight mass, they take on another quality altogether. In a communal act of worship they draw out what is personal to us—our memories, our joys, our sorrows—and make it part of something far larger and greater. Our stories become interwoven with those of our neighbours, and with the central story of the Son of God born in our midst. And as we sing those stories together it becomes both an offering to God, and a discovery of God. As the shepherds learned long ago, the glory of God can touch our lives at such moments.

Over the next two weeks we will be exploring the glory of Christmas by looking at the four songs which Luke includes in his story of Jesus' birth: Mary's Magnificat, Zechariah's Benedictus, the Gloria of the angelic host, and Simeon's Nunc Dimittis. (The traditional titles come from the opening words of the songs in Latin.) Although Luke describes them as being spoken rather than sung, they strongly resemble the hymns and sacred songs of the Jewish scriptures. It seems that Luke consciously used this style as a way of bringing the past, present and future together. The songs remember Israel's longing for salvation, and their dreams of a better world. They celebrate the way this is coming to fruition in the birth of the long-awaited Messiah. And they look forward to a world trans-formed by the knowledge of God's saving love for all people.

These are songs of praise. But they are also songs of prophecy, which challenge us to work for the transformation of our own world until the justice and peace of God become a reality for everyone.

These notes are based on the New Revised Standard Version (NRSV), but they may be used with any version of the Bible.

The Magnificat and the Benedictus

1 The Magnificat: setting the scene

Luke 1:26–38

Reading the annunciation scene as a prelude to the Magnificat can shed new light on a familiar story. Several key themes are established early on. First, the 'favour' of God is declared to Mary (vv. 28, 30). As we shall see, this idea dominates all four songs, and the circle of favour is enlarged at every stage until it includes everyone, Jew and Gentile alike. The arrival of the Messiah is not a judgment on humanity, but rather an expression of God's continuing delight with us. The creator continues to look on all that is made, and finds it good. No wonder Mary rejoices.

Second, the promises of God are being fulfilled in a surprising way. The Saviour of the world will grow secretly in Mary's womb, his great-ness framed and shaped by her humility (vv. 31–33). The Magnificat—and indeed the rest of the Gospel—will celebrate this irony again and again, as conventional notions of power and greatness are completely overturned in Jesus' life and teaching. The Messiah from the house of David was expected to repeat David's successes, winning great military victories which would re-establish Israel as the powerful and prosperous nation they had once been. Yet this son of David would usher in a very different kind of kingdom, the kingdom of peace prophesied in Isaiah 9:7, rooted in the justice and righteousness of God.

The other central theme is the greatness of God. Here God is named as the Most High, the Lord (vv. 32, 35)—again, terms that contrast sharply with the lowly circumstances of the child's birth. This is the God that Mary will celebrate in song. Our word for worship is derived from the Old English *weorthscipe*, reflecting the 'worth' of the one who is worshipped. As Mary shows, true worship involves obedience as well as praise, for only then do we allow God to be God. Her voluntary surrender to the will of God will be mirrored later in the Gospel as her son wrestles with his fears in Gethsemane (22:42).

2 The Magnificat: celebrating the greatness of God

Luke 1:46–50

'My soul magnifies the Lord!' As we saw yesterday, worship defines our relationship with God. God is great, and is 'made great' (the literal meaning of the Greek word) by our praise. But where does that leave us? It is important not to let our own sense of unworthiness prevent us enjoying God's gifts.

Mary finds the right balance. Although she acknowledges her lowly state, she recognizes and fully accepts the grace of God for what it is. God has looked on her with favour (v. 48) and done great things for her (v. 50). And if all generations should call her blessed as a result, so be it. How do we feel about the blessings we enjoy? And how is that reflected, both in our prayers and in our lives?

In hymns of this style, the opening declaration of praise is swiftly followed by a statement setting out the reasons for it (vv. 49–50). Two particular qualities of God are identified here—holiness and mercy—and they form another theme which Luke develops carefully in his Gospel. He is particularly fond of stories which seem to contrast the two virtues: Simon the Pharisee and the woman who anoints Jesus' feet (7:36–50); the two brothers in the story of the Prodigal Son (15:11–32); the Pharisee and the tax collector (18:9–14). In each case, the presence of mercy exposes the 'holiness' as a false and narrow self-righteousness. In reality, the holiness of God is merciful, and the mercy of God is holy.

These are not only moral attributes. As Psalm 111 shows, Jewish thought often linked both qualities with concrete acts of liberation:

The Lord is gracious and merciful:
he provides food for those who fear him. (Psalm 111:4–5)

He sent redemption to his people;
he has commanded his covenant forever:
holy and awesome is his name. (Psalm 111:9)

We shall see tomorrow how Mary continues to explore this theme.

23

3 The Magnificat: celebrating the new world order

Luke 1:51–55

As the song moves outwards in scope, Mary's own experience becomes a key to exploring the wider activity of God. God has always intervened to help the lowly (vv. 51–52). The Greek verbs speak of decisive action in the past. Although no specific examples are given, the song echoes those psalms which celebrate Israel's exodus from Egypt and other occasions of deliverance (e.g. Psalms 114, 118, 137). There are also clear parallels with Hannah's song in 1 Samuel 2:1–10.

This is where the prophetic tone of the Magnificat comes to the fore. Like Hannah, Mary sets up a series of comparisons which celebrate the radical displacement of the proud, powerful and wealthy in favour of the poor and powerless (vv. 52–53). Again, this is seen in very concrete terms: 'God has lifted up the lowly; he has filled the hungry with good things, and sent the rich away empty.' Despite Luke's use of the past tense, this will also be a hallmark of Jesus' ministry (see 9:12–17, 18:18–25) and of the continuing ministry of his followers (see 14:7–14).

As Mary says, the promises of God are there for every generation (vv. 54–55). So how can we implement that radical vision in our own age? At a time of year when the gulf between rich and poor can be all too apparent, how will we respond to the real needs around us?

These can be uncomfortable questions in a relatively wealthy society. But Mary's song reminds us that our individual experience of God cannot be separated from the overall vision of justice, health and peace that is promised in the kingdom of God.

4 The Benedictus: setting the scene

Luke 1:5–25, 39–45, 57–66

As the length of today's reading illustrates, Luke attaches great importance to the story of John's birth. But it is clear at every stage that John is the forerunner, not the main act. Even though he will be 'great in the sight of the Lord' and 'filled with the Holy Spirit' (v. 15), his main task will be to 'make ready a people prepared for the Lord' (v. 17—the prophecy of Isaiah 40:3).

This is a prophetic role. In this respect, John is likened both to Samuel, who prepared the way for David, and to Elijah, who was expected to return before the Messiah came. Like Samuel, John will be born to a barren woman, and abstain from strong drink (see 1 Samuel 1:1–11); like Elijah, he will preach the way of righteousness, and 'turn the hearts of parents to their children'. According to Malachi 4:5–6 this would herald the 'great and terrible day of the Lord'. Although John's preaching will reflect this note of judgment, it will do so in order to prompt repentance (see 3:7–9). Gabriel's message is 'good news' (v. 19).

The similarities between the two stories—the appearance of Gabriel, the miraculous conceptions, the giving of names—allow us to contrast the reactions of Zechariah, Elizabeth and Mary, and learn from their experience. Zechariah's doubts are understandable; like Abraham and Sarah (Genesis 17:16–17) he finds it difficult to believe that a son can be born to such elderly parents. Yet to their great joy it is true. Elizabeth rejoices immediately (vv. 25, 41–45), and her joy and her grasp of the situation clearly help both Mary (vv. 36–38) and Zechariah (vv. 60–63). Experiences of God are given to be shared.

Zechariah regains his speech only when he insists that the child is named John, in fulfilment of the angel's command (vv. 13, 63). It is his act of obedience which sets him free to glorify God (v. 64).

5 The Benedictus: celebrating the faithfulness of God

Luke 1:67–75

Zechariah's song begins where Mary's ends, celebrating the fulfilment of God's promises to Israel. In a sense, the song is about the future. As he promised, God has now raised up a Saviour from the house of David (vv. 69–70). Yet this is interpreted according to the great acts of salvation that Israel has known in the past.

Again, the exodus is seen as the central event. This is where the people were most dramatically redeemed (v. 68) and saved from their enemies (v. 71). As we can see from Psalm 106, the ancient songs of Israel looked back to this moment in times of trouble, and found in it a reminder of God's constant love and loyalty:

He rebuked the Red Sea, and delivered them
from the hand of the enemy. (Psalm 106:9–10)

Many times he delivered them, and showed compassion
according to the abundance of his steadfast love. (Psalm 106:43–45)

Zechariah traces the roots of this steadfast love back to God's covenant with Abraham (vv. 72–73). As Genesis 17:1–10 makes clear, a covenant involves a pledge by both parties. Here, the response to God's saving initiative is that we should 'serve him without fear, in holiness and righteousness before him all our days' (vv. 74–75). For Zechariah, a temple priest, this would naturally involve formal worship (the Greek verb carries the sense of priestly service).

This is an important theme for Luke, who begins and ends his story in the temple. But there are also implications for our life in the world. This time holiness is linked with righteousness, or justice (the same Greek word may mean both)—and it is this aspect of God's promise that will be addressed in tomorrow's reading.

6 The Benedictus: celebrating the dawn

Luke 1:76–79

For two verses Zechariah focuses on the role his son will play in the unfolding drama. He will be the prophet of the Most High (v. 76), the one preparing the way for the Lord. As we saw earlier, this refers back to the prophecy of Isaiah 40:3, but the same idea also appears in Malachi 3:1 concerning the anticipated return of Elijah.

All the Gospels go out of their way to stress that John is not the Messiah, which suggests that there may have been confusion or conflict at some point. Luke makes the point very simply: John is the prophet of the Most High, whereas Jesus is the Son of the Most High (v. 32).

John's role will be an important one, however, for he will 'give knowledge of salvation to his people by the forgiveness of their sins' (v. 77). Luke is very different from Matthew in this respect. In Matthew, John calls people to repentance, and baptizes them as they make their confession (3:1–6). The implication is that Jesus alone can forgive sins. Yet Luke follows Mark in making John an agent of forgiveness as well (see Mark 1:4). As the Jewish scriptures remind us, it is God who forgives sins, as he has always done: 'To the Lord our God belong mercy and forgiveness' (Daniel 9:9).

The Messiah's role and purpose is broader than that. As Zechariah outlines it in verses 78–79, it is a blaze of light into a world darkened by suffering and death. The image comes from Isaiah 9:2, where the prophet looks forward to an endless kingdom of peace, freedom and justice. We will hear more about peace next week, when we look at the angels' song. In the meantime, it is important that those who dwell in darkness and the shadow of death should not be forgotten at Christmas. In our prayers and in our actions, how can we help bring the light of Christ to them?

Guidelines

As we have seen this week, both the Magnificat and the Benedictus celebrate the divine plan of salvation that is coming to fruition in Christ. In the midst of their celebration, however, they examine closely what that salvation really means. This is why the harsh realities of life are never far from the surface. Poverty and hunger, suffering and death—this is where people need salvation, in the real issues which confront them in their day-to-day lives.

Later in the Gospel, Jesus will make the same point about himself by reading out Isaiah 61:1–2 and declaring, 'Today this scripture has been fulfilled in your hearing' (4:16–21). The poor will hear good news; the captive will be released; the blind will see, and the oppressed will go free. The child in these songs and the firebrand in the synagogue at Nazareth are one and the same person.

Sadly, some of our Christmas songs can be cloyingly sentimental, and lead us away from that kind of vision of reality. But the best songs bring together the deepest needs of the world and the highest hopes of heaven, and as they do so, they encourage us to look for the glory of God in both places:

> Yet with the woes of sin and strife
> The world has suffered long;
> Beneath the angel-strain have rolled
> Two thousand years of wrong;
> And man at war with man, hears not
> The love-song which they bring:
> O hush the noise, ye men of strife,
> And hear the angels sing.
> EDMUND SEARS (1810–76)

(Next week's Guideline suggests listening to some of the ways in which these four songs have been set to music. No particular composers are recommended, as musical tastes vary so widely. The idea is that you should find something which inspires you. You may already have your own favourites, but if not, you may like to spend some time in a library or record shop this week, sampling some of the options.)

The Gloria and the Nunc Dimittis

1 The Gloria: setting the scene

Luke 2:1–7

Such are the purposes of God that even the emperor of Rome unknowingly plays his part in the drama of salvation. According to Luke, Augustus' census ensures that Jesus is born in Bethlehem, the ancient home of the house of David (see Micah 5:2).

'He will be great, and will be called the Son of the Most High, and the Lord God will give to him the throne of his ancestor David' (1:32). Gabriel's words have prepared us for a royal birth, surrounded with awe and wonder and majesty. Yet the reality could not be more prosaic. Mary's labour comes quickly; the town is full; and the incarnate Son of God must spend his first night in an animals' feeding trough.

'Foxes have holes, and birds have nests; but the Son of Man has nowhere to lie down and rest' (9:58). Luke makes much of Jesus' homelessness. Even in death, he will be laid in a stranger's tomb (23:50–53). And yet he is not without comfort. Then, as now, he will be wrapped in cloth by those who love him. That simple act speaks volumes about the mystery of the incarnation. First, the Son of God experienced human need. As the figure of Solomon comments in the apocryphal book of Wisdom: 'I was nursed with care in swaddling cloths. For no king ever had a different beginning of existence. There is for all one entrance into life and one way out' (Wisdom 7:4–6).

Second, and more significant, he also experienced those needs being met. The source of all love knew what it was to be loved, not only by God, but by the people who filled his life.

The needs of that new and highly vulnerable baby remind us of those in our own world who are in need of shelter, warmth and comfort. In a sense, providing financial or prayerful support is the easy option. It is much harder to provide practical, tangible help; and yet that is what this story challenges us to do.

2 The Gloria: celebrating the glory and peace of God

Luke 2:8–14

The true splendour and majesty of Jesus' birth, hidden in yesterday's reading, now bursts out as the angel appears to the startled shepherds. As glory of the Lord shone around them (v. 9), the message of salvation is announced. The universal 'good news of great joy for all the people' (v. 10) is also directed personally to the shepherds: 'to you is born this day' (v. 11). The child is not just a Saviour; he is their Saviour—and ours, too.

Jesus is also described as the Messiah, and the Lord. Luke may simply be stringing the different titles together, just as he did in 1:32–33, to denote Jesus' overwhelming greatness. But it is possible that the titles follow a deliberate sequence: Jesus is hailed as the Saviour of particular individuals or groups, like the shepherds; he is hailed as the Messiah of Israel, the Chosen One for the chosen people of God; and he is hailed in universal terms as the Lord of all.

This sense of an ever-widening picture continues as the angelic host lift their voices in praise: 'Glory to God in the highest heaven, and on earth peace among those whom he favours!' While the earlier songs had spoken of God's favour resting on Mary (1:48), and on Israel (1:68), this time there are no limits. The God of highest heaven is the God of the whole earth; and the peace of God is offered to everyone through the gift of this child.

As we saw last week, this peace (in Hebrew, *shalom*) includes justice and righteousness (Isaiah 9:1–7), but that is only part of the vision sketched out in the early chapters of Isaiah. True *shalom* also embraces political harmony (Isaiah 2:4), economic harmony (3:13–23), and social and ecological harmony (11:1–9). Here again, the song of praise is a song of prophecy, setting out the transformative quality of the kingdom which is dawning in Christ.

3 Reactions to the Gloria

Luke 2:15–20

The shorter songs this week allow us to see how the leading characters in the story respond to all they have seen and heard.

Recognizing that 'the Lord' has spoken to them through the angels' words, the shepherds set off for Bethlehem immediately (v. 15). Unlike the disciples who witness Jesus' transfiguration (9:28–36), they have no desire to hold on to the glimpse of glory they have experienced. It has been enough. In all that glory, they have recognized that the focal point is something far more mundane—a child wrapped in cloth, lying in a manger (v. 12)—and that is what they hasten to find (v. 16).

As the shepherds repeat the angel's message to Mary and Joseph (v. 17), they offer a classic model of evangelism. Quite literally, they are handing on the 'good news' they have received (v. 10), news which amazes everyone who hears it (v. 18). Luke will record a similar sense of amazement many times as Jesus' ministry gets under way (see, for example, 4:22, 32, 36).

Mary seems less amazed (v. 19)—presumably because she has already heard the good news from both Gabriel and Elizabeth. None the less, she treasures the shepherds' words, and ponders them in her heart. Luke's portrait of Mary is very reflective at this point. It is an invitation to the reader to meditate on the angels' message, to think about the meaning of Christ's birth, to explore its implications in our own day and age. Mary has already proved herself to be an outstandingly receptive and faithful disciple, and yet even she has more to learn. As we read again the familiar words of the Christmas story, may we too find fresh meaning in it.

4 The Nunc Dimittis: setting the scene

Luke 2:21–28

Luke is keen to show how Jesus' parents comply with the requirements of Jewish law, so Jesus is circumcised and named (after eight days, as in Leviticus 12:3), and Mary is purified (presumably after 40 days, as in Leviticus 12:1–8). However, the purification seems to be conflated with another ritual, where Jesus is presented to the Lord. This may be modelled on the consecration of the first-born required by Exodus 13:2. But it is interesting that Luke does not mention the ritual 'buying back' of the first-born which is stipulated later in that chapter.

Again, there are echoes of the story of Hannah and Samuel (1 Samuel 1:11, 24–38)—Mary and Joseph do not buy back their son, because they are handing him over to God. When Jesus later speaks of his 'father's house' on another visit to the temple (v. 49), it will be transparently clear whose child he is.

It is a huge sacrifice on Mary and Joseph's part, and its full significance will only begin to emerge as Simeon speaks of the child's future (vv. 34–35). We will look more closely at that in two days' time, but it is important to note here that the faithful obedience shown by Mary and Joseph applies equally to the law of Moses (v. 22), and to the word of God which Gabriel has spoken (1:31, 35).

From verse 25, the focus switches to Simeon. Among the many qualities Luke mentions, it is his openness to the Holy

Spirit—mentioned three times—which stands out. In traditional Jewish thought, this marked him out as a prophet (see, for example, 1 Samuel 10:10–12), and his specific prophetic role was to recognize the Messiah (v. 26). As this suggests, speech is only one aspect of prophecy. The gift of discernment is equally important—the ability to be in the right place at the right time; the ability to see things for what they are; the ability to recognize in them the hand and voice of God. How can we be more open to the Spirit in all these things?

5 The Nunc Dimittis: celebrating the revelation of God

Luke 2:28–32

As Simeon takes the Christ-child in his arms, there is a profound moment of recognition. The Spirit's promise—that Simeon would not see death until he had seen the Lord's Messiah—is now fulfilled (v. 26).

· The granting of that promise means Simeon's song begins on a slightly strange note. It is a song of praise, as Luke points out (v. 28), and yet the first thing Simeon praises God for is the fact that he can now die. We do not know how old he was, or how long he had waited, but what is clear from verse 29 is the deep sense of peace that he feels at the prospect. This, too, is part of the shalom of God.

In the same verse, Simeon uses the traditional Greek words for master and slave to describe his relationship with God. It is a mark of the devotion which Luke has already mentioned (v. 25), but it also illustrates why he has such peace. Like Mary and Zechariah before him, he is content to allow God to be God, in death as well as life.

The song moves on to explore the hope of salvation encapsulated in this tiny child. Based on an earlier prophecy of Isaiah, that hope is explicitly universal: 'The Lord has bared his holy arm before the eyes of all the nations; and all the ends of the earth shall see the salvation of our God' (Isaiah 52:10).

It is this child who will be the light (v. 32), bringing revelation to the Gentiles, and glory to Israel. In this context, revelation and glory appear to have the same meaning—Jews and Gentiles alike will see in Christ the presence of God, and be saved by it.

The breadth of Simeon's vision is thought-provoking. Is everyone saved, simply because this child has been born? Or is there more to it than that? However we answer these questions, it is important to hear the hope and confidence of Simeon's song.

6 Reactions to the Nunc Dimittis

Luke 2:33–35

It is difficult to know why Mary and Joseph are 'amazed' at Simeon's words (v. 33), given all they have seen and heard before. Perhaps it is the universalism of his vision; perhaps it is just the coincidence of yet another stranger recognizing who their son is. In fact, what follows seems more remarkable, because it is here we get our first glimpse of the future that lies in store for this child.

Simeon offers a mixed blessing, to say the least (vv. 34–35). When he speaks of Jesus being 'destined for the falling and rising of many in Israel', it is clear that his ministry will have a disturbing and unsettling effect. The image may stem from Isaiah 8:14–15, where the prophet speaks of Israel falling down after knocking against the stumbling-block of God. Later, Luke connects this idea with Psalm 118:22: 'What then does this text mean, "The stone that the builders rejected has become the chief cornerstone."? Everyone who falls on that stone will be broken to pieces' (Luke 20:17–18).

The sheer fact of Jesus forces people to choose. Is he the Messiah, or is he not? Many will oppose him, and all will find their thoughts revealed as the 'light'—Simeon's term for Christ (v. 32)—shines into their hearts. Yet according to his prophecy they will also rise. Ultimately, it seems to be a hopeful message for the people of Israel.

For Mary, however, it is a dark and difficult message: 'A sword will pierce your own soul too'. Her son will also have his falling before he discovers what it is to rise. This could refer to the rejection which Simeon has just mentioned; it could also refer to his ultimate fate. Even at this early stage, the shadow of the cross is glimpsed in the narrative.

Guidelines

After so many words, it is time we allowed the music of these songs to speak to us. Whatever song(s) you have chosen, in whatever setting, play them several times, and allow yourself to hear in the music some of the hopes, the dreams and the glory we have thought about for the last two weeks. If you find your thoughts wandering into other areas of life, stay with those thoughts, for there too the glory of God can break through in our midst.

Music can be a discovery of God. It can also be our offering to God. Above all, let the music help you rejoice in the story of the Saviour's birth. And as we stand on the threshold of a new year, let it help you celebrate the dawning of God's reign of peace throughout our world.

> *For lo! the days are hastening on,*
> *By prophet bards foretold,*
> *When with the ever-circling years,*
> *Comes round the age of gold;*
> *When peace shall over all the earth*
> *Its ancient splendours fling,*
> *And the whole world give back the song*
> *Which now the angels sing.*
> EDMUND SEARS (1810–76)

FURTHER READING

Richard Burridge, *Four Gospels—One Jesus?*, SPCK, 1994

Robert C. Tannehill, *The Narrative Unity of Luke–Acts*, Fortress, 1986

New Daylight

New Daylight is ideal for those looking for a devotional approach to reading and understanding the Bible. Each issue covers four months of daily Bible readings and reflection from a regular team of contributors, who have represented a stimulating mix of church backgrounds, from Baptist to Anglican Franciscan. Each day's reading provides a Bible passage (text included), helpful comment and prayer or thought for reflection. In *New Daylight* the Sundays and special festivals from the Church calendar are noted on the relevant days, offering a chance to get acquainted with the rich traditions of the Christian year. Our *New Daylight* extract includes readings for Christmas (from the September–December 2002 notes) and also a taster of readings from Esther. Both are written by Jenny Robertson, who has lived and worked for a number of years in Russia and has written many books for both adults and children, including *Strength of the Hills* for BRF.

Glad tidings of good things!

Awake, awake! Put on your strength, O Zion; Put on your beautiful garments, O Jerusalem, the holy city!... Shake yourself from the dust, arise... Loose yourself from the bonds of your neck, O captive daughter of Zion. For thus says the Lord: 'You have sold yourselves for nothing, And you shall be redeemed without money.'... How beautiful upon the mountains are the feet of him who brings good news, who proclaims peace, who brings glad tidings of good things, who proclaims salvation, who says to Zion, 'Your God reigns!'

The season of Advent is drawing to an end. In Russia it lasts 40 days and is kept as a fast. You certainly enjoy a turkey dinner after that—except that it's not a tradition in Russia! In the West, Advent is a time of penitence, looking forward to the one who, ever present, will also come to be our judge, as the Collect for the Fourth Sunday reminds us.

Our reading today picks up the gospel themes of conversion, redemtion, peace, new hope and great news! Advent arouses us with the joyful cry of 'Awake!' We must uncurl spiritually from safe hibernation, stretch our limbs and get ready to receive generosity on generosity, gift on gift. Like Zion, we must clear out the dust of old hurts, put on party clothes and look up because a messenger is running over the hillsides with great news. In the ancient world, the messenger who bore good news was highly valued:

'Like the cold of snow in time of harvest is a faithful messenger... he refreshes the soul of his masters' (Proverbs 25:13). Our messenger is indeed faithful, 'the Amen, the Faithful and True Witness' (Revelation 3:14). He is word-bearer and Word, the bridegroom who 'proceeding from his marriage chamber, swiftly runs his race', as the old Scottish liturgy reminds us, lifting the image from Psalm 19:5. And our messenger looked for no water to bathe his beautiful feet, but stooped and served his friends in the upper room on the night before he died.

Sunday reflection

Amid Christmas cards, mince pies and carol concerts, reflect that we are to 'make ourselves holy today and be ready, because on the morrow we shall see the splendour of God among us'.

Aberdeen Breviary

JR

In praise of the royal bridegroom

You are fairer than the sons of men; Grace is poured upon Your lips; Therefore God has blessed You forever. Gird Your sword upon Your thigh, O Mighty One, with Your glory and Your majesty. And in Your majesty ride prosperously because of truth, humility, and righteousness... You love righteousness and hate wickedness; Therefore God, Your God, has anointed You with the oil of gladness more than Your companions.

God throws lavish parties, particularly delighting in a wedding feast, and this theme runs through scripture, ending with the great marriage banquet in Revelation 21. John the Baptist refers to Jesus as 'bridegroom' (John 3:29) and Jesus uses the term to describe himself, too: 'Can the friends of the bridegroom fast while the bridegroom is with them?' (Mark 2:19).

Psalm 45 praises the bridegroom-king who, like the lover in the Song of Songs, is 'fairer than the sons of men'. He is lavishly anointed—oil in scripture often refers to the Holy Spirit, which takes us to another bridegroom passage Jesus also refers to: 'The Spirit of the Lord God is upon me, because the Lord has anointed me... He has covered me with the robe of righteousness, as a bridegroom decks himself with ornaments, And as a bride adorns herself with her jewels' (Isaiah 61:1, 10). This rich passage is woven into Jewish marriage prayers to this day. The key to the king's greatness and the bridegroom's beauty is truth, humility and righteousness (v. 4) and this is the heart of the gospel message that the baby born in Bethlehem will bring.

We saw yesterday that the coming king is compared to a bridegroom sun, whose path extends across the heavens (Psalm 19:5–6), while Malachi 4:2 promises that 'the Sun of Righteousness shall rise with healing in his wings'. In Orkney, a prehistoric burial mound is built so that, at the winter solstice, the noonday sun strikes to its heart. However, the healing rays of our bridegroom sun pierce the darkest places of our hearts. Let him shine in your sorrows and joys with beauty and healing this Christmastide.

Reflection

Christ, the light and beauty of the fabric of the world.

Aberdeen Breviary
JR

Displaced by decree

And it came to pass in those days that a decree went out from Caesar Augustus that all the world should be registered... So all went to be registered, everyone to his own city. Joseph also went up from Galilee, out of the city of Nazareth, into Judea, to the city of David, which is called Bethlehem, because he was of the house and lineage of David, to be registered with Mary, his betrothed wife, who was with child.

So they are on the way, caught in the confusion of jostling crowds. A Polish carol has Mary plead, 'Please go slowly, Joseph, I can't rush along so fast, look what a load I bear. I'm so tired, all I can think of is somewhere to stay, a nice little inn.' Yet 'there was no room for them in the inn' (Luke 2:7).

The rulers of the world pass decrees and people are displaced. In 1939, thousands of Poles were transported to Siberia. Families were torn apart. A Polish boy placed in a Soviet orphanage found a small compatriot. They were forbidden to keep Christmas, but the boys hid in the empty dormitory on Christmas Eve. They blew on the icy windowpane and glimpsed the Christmas star, pulled straw from their mattresses, knelt beside their 'crib' and whispered well-loved carols.

In 1945, the Allies redrew the map of Poland. People were resettled in villages where banished German-speaking people had lived for centuries. A family being transported west in an unheated wagon realized that it was Christmas Eve. 'The children were crying with hunger,' the mother said. 'Our Jan always caught trout with his bare hands for our Christmas supper and I baked cakes. But the Christ child is with us wherever we go—and suddenly we smelt the fragrant scent of a Christmas tree and saw the blaze of candles in the dark.'

Reflection

Perhaps you will keep vigil with other Christians with candles and carols. Perhaps you will be filling stockings for children too excited to sleep or caring for an elderly relative. Whatever you do, 'the wondrous gift is given' in great silence. The Aberdeen Breviary reminds us that 'the Son of God came from a secret habitation to visit and console those who desired him with all their heart'.

JR

Come, let us adore Christ the Lord!

The people who walked in darkness have seen a great light; Those who dwelt in the land of the shadow of death, upon them a light has shined... For unto us a Child is born, unto us a Son is given... 'Rain down, you heavens, from above, And let the skies pour down righteousness; let the earth open, Let them bring forth salvation, And let righteousness spring up together, I, the Lord, have created it.'

And the Word became flesh and dwelt among us, and we beheld His glory, the glory as of the only begotten of the Father, full of grace and truth.

'Christmas Day has dawned, the child is born, the Prince of Peace is here, the "Dayspring" from on high has visited us' (see Luke 1:78). 'Dully night' has passed. This phrase is Dunbar's—a poet who lived at the same time as the *Aberdeen Breviary* was compiled. 'It is midwinter but the earth blossoms with salvation' (see Isaiah 45:8). All creation celebrates. The old carols say that sparrows, robins and starlings rejoiced with country people who fed their cattle in the first light of Christmas Day, believing with simple trust that the very animals bowed their knee on the night the Lord of all was born. Even the wild ox serves the infant king in the manger (Job 39:9) and shall we not rejoice, too, this day of his birth?

We express our joy with family and friends, with food and gifts in honour of the child who makes his home among us. 'The Word became flesh and dwelt among us,' John's Gospel sings with the beauty of a single violin. 'We beheld his glory... full of grace and truth.' The words of the passage resonate with adoration. We marvel at the mystery, that the glory of the 'only begotten of the Father' is made manifest in our mortal bodies with their transient beauty, their distressing infirmities, 'full of grace and truth'.

Prayer

'Equal with the Father, you took the infirmity of our flesh to gird us with the garments of everlasting life. You shine within a stable, making night as radiant as day, for nothing could break the power of darkness until the Light of the world should dawn' (Aberdeen Breviary). *O, come let us adore him, Christ the Lord! Amen*

JR

The first fruits of harvest

Why do the nations rage, And the people plot a vain thing? The kings of the earth set themselves, And the rulers take counsel together, Against the Lord and against His Anointed… The Lord has said to Me, 'You are My Son, Today I have begotten You. Ask of Me, and I will give You the nations for Your inheritance, And the ends of the earth for Your possession.'

The gospel of peace begins in a poor outhouse. It continues on the hillsides and highways of Galilee, and then on Skull Hill outside Jerusalem. Then there is silence, darkness, a tomb—and resurrection. Then meetings and discourses, a disappearing, expectant prayer, tongues of fire, judgment—and now the nations of the world are being brought into the inheritance of the Lord's anointed.

For the day after the Lord's birthday, the liturgical year commemorates Stephen, the first martyr. This psalm, along with the other Old Testament readings we have followed, was part of Christmastide worship in the Scot-tish medieval church. Affirming Christ as the Messiah, it plunges us into the turmoil that arose when the early Church launched its message into the world. Stephen, witnessing to Christ, 'gazed into heaven and saw the glory of God, and Jesus standing at the right hand of God' (Acts 7:55). As the executioners hurled their stones, Stephen called, 'Lord Jesus receive my spirit… do not charge them with this sin' (vv. 59–60). Stephen's witness was to have a life-changing impact on the young man, Saul, who held the executioners' cumbersome outer garments. His ministry would bring the 'ends of the earth' within the possession of Christ. As we carve cold turkey, enjoy and use our Christmas presents, we recall Stephen's witness, his gift to the Lord of the Church, which is an inheritance we share to this day.

Prayer

All through the world, your Church, O Christ is adorned with purple and fine linen—the blood of the martyrs. We acknowledge them as the first fruits of harvest offered to the Lord of creation and we pray that you will have pity on your people. Grant peace to your community and shed your great mercy on our souls and on the world you have made. Amen

Eastern Orthodox liturgy, adapted

JR

Where eagles dare

'Give ear, O heavens, and I will speak... Let my teaching drop as the rain, My speech distill as the dew, As raindrops on the tender herb, And as showers on the grass. For I proclaim the name of the Lord: Ascribe greatness to our God. He is the Rock, His work is perfect... He encircled him [Israel], He instructed him, He kept him as the apple of His eye. As an eagle stirs up his nest, hovers over its young, spreading out its wings, taking them up... so the Lord alone led him.'

As a young man, Moses had claimed that he could not speak (Exodus 4:10), but now, at the end of his life, he praises God's love in a song that, in its turn, bcame woven into the medieval Christmas liturgy. Perhaps you will find a moment to read these verses in full. We may imagine them sung in plainchant by men and boys in churches whose cruciform shape, decorated walls and lofty pillars were a visual aid to even the simplest person.

God's love is protective, loving and strong. He is 'a God of truth and without injustice, Righteous and upright' (Deuteronomy 32:4). His ways are perfect yet he comes silently as showers falling on young grass. The picture moves from the silence of dew fall to the mighty eagle, tipping its young from the nest to encourage them to fly, yet circling nearby with outspread wings—a mothering image used by the Lord Jesus to describe his love for Jerusalem (Matthew 23:37). We think of the cross and Jesus with his arms outstretched to save: 'And I, if I am lifted up from the earth, will draw all peoples to myself,' he says (John 12: 2).

John the Evangelist, commemorated today, is known by the sign of the eagle. His Gospel is sometimes called 'The Way of the Eagle'. It is supremely the Gospel of the Word, who came silently, gently and as refreshingly as showers, yet full of power.

Prayer

Lord, your arms are outstretched to welcome, shelter and carry your people upwards and onwards into your love. You enfold us, yet tip us out from the cocoon of our fears. Teach us to soar. Carry us on eagle wings to the heart of your glory. Amen

JR

The lost children

An angel of the Lord appeared to Joseph in a dream, saying, 'Arise, take the young Child and His mother, flee to Egypt, and stay there until I bring you word; for Herod will seek the young Child to destroy Him.' ... Then Herod... put to death all the male children who were in Bethlehem and in all its districts, from two years and under... Then was fulfilled what was spoken by Jeremiah... 'A voice was heard in Ramah, lamentation, weeping and great mourning, Rachel weeping for her children, refusing to be comforted, because they are no more.'

Warned by an angel that their baby's life was in danger, the Holy Family fled abroad, fugitives from tyranny. Herod's murderous action was in keeping with his character. He had had three of his own sons put to death. No woman's virtue was safe with Herod and no man's life, nor the lives of little children, as we know from Matthew's Gospel.

Bethlehem, visited by angels glorifying God such a short time before, was filled with the screams of babies and the laments of their mothers. Matthew states the terrible finality of loss: the children are 'no more'. The Christian Church honoured the murdered children as 'firstfruits to God and to the Lamb' (Revelation 14:4), but condoned, and sometimes actively participated in, the killing of Jewish children for the next 2000 years.

From his hiding place, a father whose 13-year-old son had been swept on to a death train and gassed, watched families jump to their deaths from burning houses as the ghetto in Warsaw was systematically destroyed. He cried, 'Arise, beloved Mother Rachel! Look at your children now! Hurry, while there is still time, the God of Israel will listen to you, otherwise the silence of the graveyard will reign and the seed of Israel will not exist.' Miraculously, a remnant survived the almost total killing.

We sorrow for these things and today—the feast of Holy Innocents —we pray for child victims of violence, war, sexual assault and bullying, road accidents, hunger, disease, neglect and need.

Prayer

Father, in this season of your Son's birth as a defenceless child, have mercy on little ones who suffer and enfold them in your healing love. Amen

JR

Marked with the old covenant, named with the new

When they had seen him, they spread the word concerning what had been told them about this child, and all who heard it were amazed at what the shepherds said to them. But Mary treasured up all these things and pondered them in her heart. The shepherds returned, glorifying and praising God for all the things they had heard and seen, which were just as they had been told. On the eighth day, when it was time to circumcise him, he was named Jesus, the name the angel had given him before he had been conceived.

The Gospel belongs to men from the sheepfold as well as to learned astrologers and kings. The oldest carols are folk songs —this is particularly true in Poland. Even in a heavily clericalized church, Polish carols touch the hearts and lives of uneducated people, just as the primary school Nativity play fills the most unruly children with wonder.

The shepherds made public what had been revealed to them, but Mary 'treasured up all these things and pondered them in her heart' (v. 19). These words give us an insight into the character of the mother that was surely reflected later in the life of her Son. The ability to treasure and ponder deep truths is the key to spiritual wisdom, peace of mind and a calm soul.

Mary and Joseph were obedient to the Law of Moses and to the word of the angel. They have the child circumcised and name him Jesus, just as the angel had commanded (v. 21).

Giving a new baby a name is always a great event. Unlike John the Baptist's parents (Luke 1: 59–60), Mary and Joseph were in complete agreement about the baby's name. The child is marked with the sign of the old covenant and is the Saviour, whose broken body will be the sign of the new covenant, branded with scourge and spear and nails. From the cradle to the cross, the Lord is literally a marked man whose wounds carry deep meaning and healing. Let us ponder this in *our* hearts.

Sunday reflection

*Says the lover to her beloved,
'your name is like perfume
poured out' (Song of Songs 1:3).
O name of Jesus, beloved,
delightful, be honoured, loved
and adored, Holy Lord.*

JR

Sword of sorrow, fire of salvation

Now when the days of her purification according to the law of Moses were completed, they brought Him to Jerusalem to present Him to the Lord... and to offer a sacrifice according to what is said in the law of the Lord, 'A pair of turtledoves or two young pigeons.' And behold there was a man in Jerusalem whose name was Simeon, and this man was just and devout, waiting for the Consolation of Israel, and the Holy Spirit was upon him. And it had been revealed to him... that he would not see death before he had seen the Lord's Christ... when the parents brought in the child Jesus... he took Him up in his arms and blessed God.

The Church traditionally recalls that, 40 days after childbirth, Mary and Joseph offered sacrifices to the Lord. This feast marks the end of Christmas on 2 February, Candlemas. In Poland, many families only then take down Christmas trees, pack away cribs and sing carols for the last time. In mid-January my husband and I were invited into the local school to watch 'cool' 16-year-olds perform a Nativity play with great devotion.

Luke in our passage records the scene with a sense of awe that echoes down the centuries. Simeon catches sight of Mary and Joseph in the Temple and realizes that 'the consolation of Israel' is at hand. He takes the child with great thankfulness, but he prophesies judgment as well as glory, and, for Mary, 'a sword of sorrow' (vv. 34, 35). The story of salvation can never be separated from the cross. Simeon's revelation is born of prayer and holy waiting. Filled with the Spirit, he acknowledges Jesus as Saviour of the world (vv. 30, 32). However, the wonder is that 'Word made flesh' is presented to the Father for the price of a pair of turtle-doves.

The Russian Orthodox say that Simeon receives the infant Christ as Isaiah received live coals from the altar of the Lord (Isaiah 6:6), crying, 'You carry the Fire, Lord of the Light that never fades.' May we receive him in all his humility and holiness and carry him in our hearts into the New Year ahead.

Prayer

You lighten my darkness when all is dim; in the depths of my soul I hear your hymn.

Polish prayer

JR

The kiss of peace

I will hear what God the Lord will speak, For He will speak peace to His people and to His saints... Mercy and truth have met together; Righteousness and peace have kissed. Truth shall spring out of the earth, And righteousness shall look down from heaven. Yes, the Lord will give what is good; And our land will yield its increase. Righteousness shall go before Him, and shall make His footsteps our pathway.

The medieval church in Scotland chanted this psalm in its Christmas worship, adoring the mystical union of Father and Son in creation and in our lives. We are back with the messenger announcing peace (Isaiah 52:7). We are back with Moses, too, praising the Lord's justice and righteousness (Deuteronomy 32:4). For the Saviour is born and 'mercy and truth have met together' in a holy kiss. The earth 'will yield its increase'.

We carry this promise into the year ahead. Yet, often our ways are stony, our lives seem fruitless and the goodness of God seems very far away. However, Christ's Nativity assures us that it is precisely when we are far off that God meets us and brings us home. Let us receive the kiss of peace the Father gives us through the Son: 'we have peace with God through our Lord Jesus Christ' (Romans 5:1).

Sometimes God offers peace to us through other people, often in unexpected ways, but never because of our doing or deserving. A lady came up to me in Warsaw and said, 'Just where we're standing my friend was rounded up. "Run," her mother said, but the child clung to her. Her mother pushed her out of the line of captives so hard that she fell and broke her leg. She lay, shocked and sobbing, and a young man on his way to plunder abandoned Jewish homes took pity on her, tore his shirt in pieces, bound her leg, carried her home and hid her. My friend limps to this day, but lives. The push her mother gave her saved her life.'

Prayer

Father, you go before me with mercy and truth. Your footsteps are my safe pathway. May I walk your way in the year ahead and receive what is good. Amen

JR

A despot's magnificence

At that time King Xerxes... gave a banquet for all his nobles and officials. The military leaders of Persia and Media, the princes, and the nobles of the provinces were present. For a full 180 days he displayed the vast wealth of his kingdom and the splendour and glory of his majesty. When these days were over, the king gave a banquet, lasting seven days, in the enclosed garden of the king's palace.

The first banquet recorded in Esther is for military men and political leaders. Then, the king's enclosed garden is opened to the public for a sumptuous seven-day feast. The guests recline on couches of silver and gold, placed on a mosaic pavement of porphyry, marble, mother-of-pearl. Royal wine in abundance is served in golden goblets. The show points up the power of the monarch. Those splendid couches appear negatively elsewhere in the Old Testament—Amos rebukes the rich who recline on couches inlaid with ivory (Amos 6:4–7).

The wealth and opulence of Xerxes' court, the secret intrigues we meet in this book, remind me of Russia. When the communist leader Andropov died in 1984, we were in Russia and my husband and I heard the news whispered by a Baptist pastor's wife. Her husband and brother were in prison.

Later that evening, visiting another Christian believer, we blundered among the guarded palaces of the mighty and drew back as limousines with darkened windows swished by in the snow, carrying the leadership to the State funeral. We walked miles—public transport had been withdrawn, to reappear next day with black flags, proof that, in a despotic regime, the individual doesn't count. It takes enormous courage, which comes only with prayer and fasting, as we shall see, to withstand the will of such a ruler. Yet the days of communist power were numbered—and the vast empire of the Medes and Persians would soon also be eclipsed.

Our passage ends on a cliffhanger: Queen Vashti gives a separate banquet. The drama takes a new twist.

Sunday Reflection

Each Sunday, we are invited to the 'enclosed garden' of the King of kings. Royal wine is poured out in abundance. Pause to remember victims of tyranny. Especially today, we recall the suffering of the Holocaust.

JR

'No end of disrespect and discord'

On the seventh day, when King Xerxes was in high spirits from wine, he commanded the seven eunuchs... to bring before him Queen Vashti... Queen Vashti refused to come. Then the king... spoke with the wise men and... Memucan replied... 'Queen Vashti has done wrong.... Therefore, if it pleases the king, let him issue a royal decree... that Vashti is never again to enter the presence of King Xerxes. Also let the king give her royal position to someone else who is better than she.'

It's not clear why Vashti refused the king's command to 'display her beauty to the people' (v. 11). Fearing that she set a precedent, the astrologers advised the king to depose his queen. The sages foresaw chaos if Vashti's bad example were to be followed by wives everywhere, so couriers were sent throughout the empire 'proclaiming in each people's tongue that every man should be ruler over his own household' (v. 22). Footnotes add that the husband's native tongue should be preferred over the wife's. Mixed marriages were an issue for Ezra and Nehemiah, too—Nehemiah curses men whose children couldn't speak the language of Judah (Nehemiah 13:24–26). Yet, consider how awkward home life becomes when mothers cannot nurture their infants in their own language. We pass on to our children the baby-talk our own mothers used. Julian of Norwich writes that a mother's service is the most intimate and most like Christ's, whose deep wisdom is our mothering. Yet power is always reflected in language and language is one of the most undervalued God-given gifts in our possession.

Today's passage points up the capricious nature of the king—jovial after wine, furious when frustrated. His son will style himself 'king of kings' (Ezra 7:12). The season of Epiphany proclaims that Jesus is 'king of kings and lord of lords' (Revelation 19:16). He says, 'Whoever comes to me I will never drive away' (John 6:37). Whatever joys or difficulties lie ahead, we enter this New Year with that sure promise.

Reflection

The petulance of the tyrant king contrasts with the pity of Christ. The opulence of Xerxes' court contrasts with the poverty of our king, Jesus, who had 'nowhere to lay his head' (Luke 9:58).

JR

Esther: lovely in form and features

Later when the anger of King Xerxes had subsided, he remembered Vashti… Then the king's personal attendants proposed, 'Let a search be made for beautiful young virgins… let the girl who pleases the king be queen instead of Vashti.' … Now there was in the citadel of Susa a Jew of the tribe of Benjamin, named Mordecai… who… had a cousin named Hadassah… also known as Esther.

Anxious to divert the despot, his servants propose an empire-wide beauty competition that, not surprisingly, delights the king and brings on stage Mordecai and Esther. It is significant for the unfolding of the drama that Mordecai, like King Saul, belongs to the tribe of Benjamin. Mordecai and Esther, like most minorities in hostile regimes, live circumspectly, taking Persian names as well as Jewish ones. Many Jews in Russia also often have two names. Their identity cards are marked, making it easier to discriminate against them. Friends there tell of almost everyday incidents of racial harassment and fear.

Hadassah won the first round of the contest and was taken to the king's palace. She may win the next round also and be chosen by the king for a night in his bed or she may not. Thereafter he might never send for her again. You might recall Abishag, the beautiful girl from Shunem, who was employed to 'lie beside' the aged King David and keep him warm (1 Kings 1:2). You might also recall Joseph, Daniel and Shadrach, Meshach and Abednego (Daniel 1:6, 7), young people of integrity brought, like Esther, into a world of intrigue and murder. God protected each of them and used them for his glory—and so it is with Esther.

The eunuch Hegai took a particular liking to her. He provided her with seven maids, special quarters and special food—a sign of particular favour. Esther doesn't refuse food forbidden by the Law or reveal her family background, but the God of Israel blesses her and she 'won the favour of everyone who saw her' (v. 15).

Reflection

Rahab the prostitute is numbered among the great names of faith (Hebrews 11:31). Pray for those trapped in prostitution and pornography, especially children, that God will shine his light into their darkness.

JR

Chosen to be queen

Now the king was attracted to Esther... and she won his favour and approval more than any of the other virgins. So he set a royal crown on her head and made her queen instead of Vashti. And the king gave a great banquet, Esther's banquet, for all his nobles and officials. He proclaimed a holiday throughout the provinces and distributed gifts with royal liberality.

Esther's compliance is mentioned twice (vv. 10 and 15). During the year of her special beauty treatments, she was strictly confined, but Mordecai did not abandon her: 'Every day he walked to and fro near the courtyard of the harem' (v. 11).

In my Warsaw courtyard looms a high brick wall, a remnant of the wartime ghetto that enclosed 450,000 people as prisoners in their own city. The feeling of being cut off and abandoned was horrifying. The few escapees were those whose contact with former friends outside the wall sustained them. Yet, even so, the cost of survival was so enormous and the risks of betrayal so high that some preferred to return to the ghetto and die with their families.

Perhaps Esther's seven maids liaised between her and Mordecai. The contact must have meant everything to her, enabling her to submit patiently to Hegai's decisions when the day came for her to go to the king (v. 15). I have noticed that young people who don't seek the public eye, but do the dull jobs no one wants behind the scenes and also unselfishly care for troubled friends are the ones who are later entrusted with leadership. A friend of mine who has risen to the top of his profession still cuts the church grass and paints the walls. A medieval poem includes patience among the Beatitudes and Esther's quiet trust is honoured. Four years have passed since Vashti was deposed. Xerxes has lost two major battles but now he chooses his new queen and hosts a third magnificent banquet in Esther's honour.

Reflection

'Delight yourself in the Lord and he will give you the desires of your heart. Commit your way to the Lord; trust in him and he will… make your righteousness shine like the dawn, the justice of your cause like the noonday sun.'
(Psalm 37:4–6)

JR

PBC INTRODUCTION

BRF's *People's Bible Commentary* series is planned to cover the whole Bible, with a daily readings approach that brings together both personal devotion and reflective study. Combining the latest scholarship with straightforward language and a reverent attitude to Scripture, it aims to instruct the head and warm the heart. The authors come from around the world and across the Christian traditions, and offer serious yet accessible commentary. The series is an invaluable resource for first-time students of the Bible, for all who read the Bible regularly, for study group leaders, and anyone involved in preaching and teaching Scripture. Volumes are published twice a year, and the series is scheduled for completion in 2005.

The General Editors for the series are the Revd Dr Richard A. Burridge, New Testament scholar and Dean of King's College, London; Dom Henry Wansbrough OSB, Master of St Benet's Hall, Oxford and Editor of The New Jerusalem Bible; Canon David Winter, writer, broadcaster and Consulting Editor for BRF's *New Daylight* Bible reading notes.

Our PBC extracts in this sampler are from *Matthew* by John Proctor, a minister of the United Reformed Church who teaches New Testament in the Cambridge Theological Federation, and *Psalms 73—150* by the late Donald Coggan, Archbishop of Canterbury from 1974 to 1980.

PBC EXTRACTS

MATTHEW 2:1–12

WORSHIP FROM AFAR

Matthew's first chapter has told of a Jewish king, born of Jewish descent, according to the promises of Jewish scriptures. That raises an intriguing question. Has Israel not got a king already? If so, what will the old king and the new have to do with each other?

The Gospel begins to answer that question by telling us (v. 1) that 'in the time of King Herod... Jesus was born in Bethlehem of Judea'. Herod was a notoriously ruthless king, with grand ambitions and a paranoid fear of any possible rival. The reader expects an ugly clash. Yet this clash comes about in an unexpected way, as light and worship stream into the story from two quite new directions.

Travelling light

The word 'magi' means possessors of mysterious wisdom or hidden knowledge. They are 'wise men', not 'kings', and the text does not mention how many they were, only that they gave three gifts. Here they represent the wealth and wisdom of the Gentile world, the deep yearning and generous worship of the nations beyond Israel, coming to greet God's royal Messiah.

As the magi represent the praise of the Gentiles, the leading of the star suggests that even creation worships. The lights of heaven rise to greet the birth of the Christ, to hail the coming of God's creative love in human flesh. The nations and the skies are moved to worship. How will Israel and her king respond?

We two kings

Herod hears of the child's birth from the magi (v. 2), and apparently wishes to worship too (v. 8). But his deeper reaction is hostile and fearful. He is disturbed and troubled, he gathers his religious leaders for advice, and his plans for action are discreet and devious. Threat, foreboding and danger are in the air, and no one (except the magi, v. 12) does anything to thwart or divert the king. Gentiles can see the reality of Christ's birth, yet Israel seems curiously unaware, while her leader tries to destroy him.

For those who know the gospel story, there are uncomfortable similarities with the events of the Passion. Jesus is called 'king of the Jews' (v. 2; 27:37). Israel's leaders gather against him (v. 4; 27:1). There are secret plots (v. 7; 26:4, 14–16). The end of the Gospel is foreshadowed in its beginning. Yet even now the wrath of men does not achieve all it plans. God is in control (v. 12), and Jesus' life is secure in his hands.

Threads of prophecy

Much of Matthew's Gospel is like woven cloth. As the lines of the story lead forward, across them run strands from scripture. The narrative is dense with echoes of and allusions to Old Testament themes.

The direct quotation in verse 6, from Micah 5:2, presents Jesus as a new David, born at Bethlehem to be shepherd king for God's people—and that royal theme will be important right through Matthew. Yet surely in this chapter we hear also an echo of Isaiah 60, which speaks of light rising in Israel and Gentiles gathering with gifts: a new era has come, an age of light and hope. Psalm 72 tells of Israel's ideal king, to whom the nations will bring worship and gifts. Numbers 24:17 prophesies the coming of a messianic figure, as the rising of a new star.

Matthew (who knew the Hebrew scriptures better than we do) would have been well aware of these echoes and of the hints they conveyed. His tapestry is rich and whole precisely because of this intersecting weave. He shows us meaning in the story by the light of the scriptures.

But is it all i-magi-nation?

So how could these events have actually happened? For myself, I am intrigued by some Iranian traditions which seem to match this story from the other end of the journey; impressed by some recent and serious astronomical enquiry into the nature of a planetary conjunction in 7BC and of a comet in 5BC; and inclined to think that improbable events become a little more probable when God's Son is born.

But I realize that this account of a wandering star and visiting foreign academics strikes some modern people as far-fetched and incredible. If that is your view, don't overlook the points of Matthew's story: that the coming of Jesus is important enough for nations and creation to honour him, for tyrant thrones to tremble, and for all the glories of scripture to be recalled.

For thought

'The hinge of all history hangs on the door of a Bethlehem stable.'
Anon

LESSONS FROM A GREAT TEACHER

In this long psalm we can see a great teacher at work. He is clearly in a position of some authority—he addresses his audience as 'my people' (v. 1). He is concerned that Israel's history should be preserved: tradition, the handing down of a nation's story, its customs and its life, can easily become corrupt. It matters. But this psalm is far more than a history lesson. It is a meditation on the significance of the story—a saga of events told in such a way that succeeding generations will see its meaning and pass it on to their successors (vv. 4–6). God has made known his nature and will; those who listen to the teaching are trustees of the truth for the generations to come.

There can be no doubt about the central figure in this saga. It is God himself. God is presented as a God of judgment and of faithfulness to his declared will. Israel is presented as a people often faithless, fickle in their allegiance to God, and regardless of the destiny which their Creator has in mind.

The language used to describe God—his patience tried (v. 18), his anger blazing (vv. 21, 31), spreading death (vv. 31, 34), sending plagues (vv. 43ff.), unleashing blazing anger, wrath, enmity and raage (v. 49), offensive as it must seem to those whose picture of God is seen through the life and teaching of Jesus—is to a degree softened within this psalm by reference to God's mercy (v. 38), his consideration for our frailty (v. 39), and his pastoral care (vv. 52ff.). If you want a case of anthropomorphism (speaking of God in human language), verse 65 will be hard to beat—the comparison of the Lord to a sleeper who wakes or a warrior who has had too much to drink. A poet must be allowed his measure of licence!

A suggestion

If readers of this book find that their knowledge of the Old Testament has grown rusty, or realize that the Old Testament is more or less uncharted territory as far as they are concerned, they could undergo a little refresher course by reading the passages which our psalmist clearly had in mind as he wrote of God's dealings with his people. For example, verses 5–8 would send them to Exodus 19—24; verses 12ff. to Exodus 14; verses 15–22 to Numbers 20; verses 23ff. to Exodus 16 and Numbers 11, and so on. Israel's teachers were great storytellers, dramatic in their presentation of events. Psalm 78 constitutes a warning never to forget 'the praiseworthy acts of the Lord and the wonders he has done' (v. 4).

A model

The psalm reaches its climax with the appearance of the great figure of David (vv. 67–72). The writer no doubt had in mind the choice of the shepherd-boy as recorded in 1 Samuel 16:1–13. He was the great king from whose line the Christ would come. But here no battles or conquests or achievements are mentioned—simply the shepherding of God's people. When in 1956 I preached in Bradford Cathedral at my own installation, I took as my text the last verse of this psalm and preached on the Prayer Book version of it: 'He fed them with a faithful and true heart and ruled them prudently with all his power.' How better could the office and work of a bishop in the Church of God be described than in this verse—or, for that matter, the calling of any leader in the Church? Here are the qualities of faithful and caring pastoral work and the exercise of discipline combined with prudence. We owe a debt of gratitude to our teacher-historian-theologian-poet man of God for giving us this model of leadership.

To ponder

We criticize our spiritual leaders. We have the right to do so. But our motto should be 'one in ten'—for every criticism ten prayers. The old Ember Day hymn suggests how we might direct our prayers:

> *Wisdom and zeal and faith impart,*
> *Firmness with meekness, from above,*
> *To bear thy people in their heart,*
> *And love the souls whom thou dost love;*
>
> *To watch and pray and never faint,*
> *By day and night their guard to keep,*
> *To warn the sinner, cheer the saint,*
> *To feed thy lambs and tend thy sheep.*

James Montgomery (1771–1854)

ADVENT AND LENT

BRF's Advent and Lent books are among the highlights of our publishing year, with well-known authors choosing their own distinctive theme around which they offer daily Bible readings, comment and points for reflection or prayer for every day in Advent and Lent. Material for group use is also included. While our Advent books are published in September, before the Christmas season begins, our Lent titles appear in November so that churches can use them when planning their Lent reading for the following spring.

Recent Lent books include *When They Crucified My Lord* by Brother Ramon SSF, *Faith Odyssey* by Richard Burridge, and *With Jesus in the Upper Room* by David Winter. Among our recent Advent books are *On the Way to Bethlehem* by Hilary McDowell, *A Candle of Hope* by Garth Hewitt, and *The Heart of Christmas* by Chris Leonard.

'SEASONS OF LIFE'

BRF also publishes books of Bible readings for people at different stages of life or in particular circumstances, as part of our regular publishing programme of adult titles. *Never Too Old to Grow* by Alexine Crawford is a book of readings for carers, combining insights from the Bible with stories of personal change and growth, drawn from the experiences of caring for people in the final 'Fourth Age' of life. By contrast, *In the Beginning* by Stephen and Jacqui Hance offers Bible insights for the first weeks of parenting, taking passages from across Scripture and exploring the simple lessons that they teach for this challenging time of life. Among other titles in this range are *Beauty from Ashes* by Jennifer Rees Larcombe (readings for times of loss), *Summer Wisdom* by Eric Rew (reflections from the book of Proverbs) and *The Best is Yet to Be* by Richard Morgan (a book of readings for older people).

HOW TO ORDER BRF NOTES

If you have enjoyed reading this sampler and would like to order the dated notes on a regular basis, they can be obtained through:

CHRISTIAN BOOKSHOPS

Most Christian bookshops stock BRF notes and books. You can place a regular order with your bookshop for yourself or for your church. For details of your nearest stockist please contact the BRF office.

INDIVIDUAL SUBSCRIPTION

For yourself

By placing an annual subscription for BRF notes, you can ensure you will receive your copy regularly. We also send you additional information about BRF: BRF News, information about our new publications and updates about our ministry activities.

You can also order a subscription for three years (two years for *Day by Day with God*), for an even easier and more economical way to obtain your Bible reading notes.

Gift subscription

Why not give a gift subscription to *New Daylight*, *Guidelines* or *Day by Day with God* to a friend or family member? Simply complete all parts of the order form and return it to us with your payment. You can even enclose a message for the gift recipient.

For either of the above, please complete the 'Individual Subscription Order Form' and send with your payment to BRF.

CHURCH SUBSCRIPTION

If you order, directly from BRF, five or more copies from our Bible reading notes range of *New Daylight*, *Guidelines* or *Day by Day with God*, they will be sent post-free. This is known as a church subscription and it is a convenient way of bulk-ordering notes for your church. There is no need to send payment with your initial order. Please complete the 'Church Subscriptions Order Form' and we will send you an invoice with your first delivery of notes.

- **Annual subscription:** you can place a subscription for a full year, receiving one invoice for the year. Once you place an annual church subscription, you will be sent the requested number of Bible reading notes automatically. You will also receive useful information to help you run your church group. You can amend your order at any time, as your requirements increase or decrease. Church subscriptions run from May to April of each year. If you start in the middle of a subscription year, you will receive an invoice for the remaining issues of the current subscription year.
- **Standing order:** we can set up a standing order for your Bible reading notes order. Approximately six to seven weeks before a new edition of the notes is due to start, we will process your order and send it with an invoice.

INDIVIDUAL & GIFT SUBSCRIPTIONS

This completed coupon should be sent with appropriate payment to BRF. Alternatively, please write to us quoting your name, address, the subscription you would like for either yourself or a friend (with their name and address), the start date and credit card number, expiry date and signature if paying by credit card.

☐ I would like to take out a subscription myself (complete name and address details only once)

☐ I would like to give a gift subscription (please complete both name and address sections below)

Your name _____

Your address _____

_____

_____ Postcode _____

Gift subscription name _____

Gift subscription address _____

_____

_____ Postcode _____

Please send beginning with the January/May/September issue: *(delete as applicable)*

(please tick box)	UK	SURFACE	AIR MAIL
New Daylight	☐ £10.50	☐ £11.85	☐ £14.10
New Daylight 3-year sub	☐ £26.50		
New Daylight LARGE PRINT	☐ £16.20	☐ £19.80	☐ £24.30
Guidelines	☐ £10.50	☐ £11.85	☐ £14.10
Guidelines 3-year sub	☐ £26.50		
Day by Day with God	☐ £11.55	☐ £12.90	☐ £15.15
Day by Day with God 2-year sub	☐ £19.99		

Total enclosed £ _____ (cheques should be made payable to 'BRF')

Payment by ☐ cheque ☐ postal order ☐ Visa ☐ Mastercard ☐ Switch

Card number: ☐☐☐☐ ☐☐☐☐ ☐☐☐☐ ☐☐☐☐ ☐☐☐☐ ☐☐☐☐

Expiry date of card: ☐☐☐☐   Issue number (Switch): ☐☐☐

Signature _____ Date / /
(essential if paying by credit/Switch card)

Please complete the payment details above and send your coupon, with appropriate payment to: BRF, First Floor, Elsfield Hall, 15–17 Elsfield Way, Oxford OX2 8FG.

Also available from your local Christian bookshop.

☐ Please do not mail me with other information about BRF

SAM0302

BRF is a Registered Charity

CHURCH SUBSCRIPTIONS

Name _____

Address _____

_____

_____ Postcode _____

Telephone Number_____

E-mail _____

Church _____

Denomination _____

Name of Minister _____

Please start my order from Jan/May/Sep* *(delete as applicable)*

I would like to pay annually/receive an invoice each issue of the notes
(delete as applicable)

Please send me:	Quantity
New Daylight	_____
New Daylight Large Print	_____
Guidelines	_____
Day by Day with God	_____

Please do not enclose payment. We have a fixed subscription year for Church Subscriptions, which is from May to April each year. If you start a Church Subscription in the middle of a subscription year, we will invoice you for the number of issues remaining in that year.

PBC ORDER FORM

Please send me the following book(s):

		Qty	Price	Total
030 8	PBC: 1 & 2 Samuel (H. Mowvley)	_____	£7.99	_____
118 5	PBC: 1 & 2 Kings (S. Dawes)	_____	£7.99	_____
070 7	PBC: Chronicles—Nehemiah (M. Tunnicliffe)	_____	£7.99	_____
031 6	PBC: Psalms 1—72 (D. Coggan)	_____	£7.99	_____
065 0	PBC: Psalms 73—150 (D. Coggan)	_____	£7.99	_____
071 5	PBC: Proverbs (E. Mellor)	_____	£7.99	_____
087 1	PBC: Jeremiah (R. Mason)	_____	£7.99	_____
028 6	PBC: Nahum—Malachi (G. Emmerson)	_____	£7.99	_____
191 6	PBC: Matthew (J. Proctor)	_____	£7.99	_____
046 4	PBC: Mark (D. France)	_____	£7.99	_____
027 8	PBC: Luke (H. Wansbrough)	_____	£7.99	_____
029 4	PBC: John (R.A. Burridge)	_____	£7.99	_____
082 0	PBC: Romans (J. Dunn)	_____	£7.99	_____
122 3	PBC: 1 Corinthians (J. Murphy-O'Connor)	_____	£7.99	_____
073 1	PBC: 2 Corinthians (A. Besançon Spencer)	_____	£7.99	_____
012 X	PBC: Galatians and 1 & 2 Thessalonians (J. Fenton)	_____	£7.99	_____
047 2	PBC: Ephesians—Colossians & Philemon (M. Maxwell)	_____	£7.99	_____
119 3	PBC: Timothy, Titus and Hebrews (D. France)	_____	£7.99	_____
092 8	PBC: James—Jude (F. Moloney)	_____	£7.99	_____

POSTAGE AND PACKING CHARGES				
order value	UK	Europe	Surface	Air Mail
£7.00 & under	£1.25	£3.00	£3.50	£5.50
£7.01–£30.00	£2.25	£5.50	£6.50	£10.00
Over £30.00	free	prices on request		

Total cost of books £ _____
Postage and packing £ _____
TOTAL £ _____

Please complete the payment details below and send your coupon, with appropriate payment to: BRF, First Floor, Elsfield Hall, 15–17 Elsfield Way, Oxford OX2 8FG.

Your name _____

Your address _____

_____

_____ Postcode _____

Total enclosed £ _____ (cheques should be made payable to 'BRF')

Payment by ❏ cheque ❏ postal order ❏ Visa ❏ Mastercard ❏ Switch

Card number: ❏❏❏❏❏❏❏❏❏❏❏❏❏❏❏❏❏❏❏❏❏❏

Expiry date of card: ❏❏❏❏   Issue number (Switch): ❏❏❏

Signature _____ Date / /

(essential if paying by credit/Switch card)

Also available from your local Christian bookshop

❏ Please do not mail me with other information about BRF

BRF is a Registered Charity

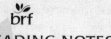

BIBLE READING NOTES

Available from your local Christian bookshop

First Floor, Elsfield Hall, 15–17 Elsfield Way,
Oxford OX2 8FG, England
Tel: 01865 319700; Fax: 01865 319701
E-mail: enquiries@brf.org.uk; Website: www.brf.org.uk

For your nearest stockist, please contact brf

Please reserve me:

	Qty
☐ New Daylight	_____
☐ New Daylight Large Print	_____
☐ Guidelines	_____
☐ Day by Day with God	_____

Name: _____

Address: _____

_____

_____

Postcode: _____

Telephone: _____

E-mail: _____

Please return this form to the bookshop below: